LONG LIVE THE KING!

Before Chadwick Boseman gained worldwide notoriety and recognition for playing T'Challa, the King of the fictional African nation Wakanda, he was known around Hollywood for being the go-to man for a biopic. Boseman was best known for his portrayal of Jackie Robinson in 42, James Brown in Get on Up, and Thurgood Marshall in Marshall.

Today, the Howard University graduate is a growing household name, by successfully breaking into the Marvel Cinematic Universe to be the first black actor to play a lead role in a superhero movie, while being a source of inspiration for African American children and children worldwide.

THE STORY OF
CHADWICK BOSEMAN
THE BLACK PANTHER

THE STORY OF
CHADWICK BOSEMAN
THE BLACK PANTHER

BY TONY ROSE

COLOSSUS BOOKS
A Division of Amber Communications Group, Inc.
New York   Phoenix   Los Angeles

WWW.AMBERBOOKSPUBLISHING.COM
WWW.TONYROSEENTERPRISES.COM

The Story of Chadwick Boseman:
The Black Panther
Published by: Colossus Books
Phoenix, Arizona

Tony Rose, Publisher / Editorial Director
Yvonne Rose, Editor

The publication is designed to provide accurate and authoritative information in regard to the subject matter covered. It is sold with the understanding that the Publisher is not engaged in rendering legal or other professional services. If legal advice or other expert assistance is required, the services of a competent professional person should be sought.

Copyright 2020 by Conant B. Rose
ISBN: 978-1-0878-0056-1
Library of Congress Control Number: 2019921114
Printed in the United States of America

CONTENTS

NOW IS HIS TIME!

After years of acting in one biopic after another, Chadwick Boseman's role as Black Panther in the "Avengers" films and the 2018 eponymous blockbuster, the ninth highest-grossing movie of all time, has established him as the rare breed of actor with star power.

In the 2019 Golden Globe Awards, "Black Panther" ended up taking home the award for Outstanding Performance by a Cast in a Motion Picture as well as Outstanding Action Performance by a Stunt Ensemble in a Motion Picture.

In his acceptance speech, Boseman touched on the significance of the film in an industry historically dominated by white actors and directors. "When I think of going to work every day and the passion and the intelligence, the resolve, the discipline, that everyone showed, I also think of two questions that we all have received during the course of multiple publicity runs."

The questions were whether they thought the film would receive the kind of reception it did and whether *Black Panther* had changed the way the industry works.

Boseman responded: "My answer to that is to be young, gifted and black... we all know what it's like to be told that there is not a place for you to be featured. Yet, you are young, gifted and black. We know what it's like to be told that there's not a screen for you to be featured on, a stage for you to be featured on. We know what it's like to be the tail and not the head. We know what it's like to be beneath and not above."

"That is what we went to work with every day, because we knew, not that we would be around during awards season or that it would make a billion dollars, but we knew that we had something special that we wanted to give the world," he continued. "That we could be full human beings in the roles that we were playing, that we could create a world that exemplified a world that we wanted to see. And to come to work every day and to solve problems with this group of people, this director, that is something that I wish all actors would get the opportunity to experience."

"If you get to experience that, you will be a fulfilled artist." Boseman wrapped up by promising a sequel: "One thing that I do know -- did it change the industry? -- is that you can't have a *Black Panther* now without a 'two' on it."

CHAPTER 1

THE BEGINNING...

Chadwick Aaron Boseman, a Sagittarian was born November 29, 1977 in The Upstate area of Anderson, South Carolina. According to his DNA test results, Chadwick's ancestors were Krio people from Sierra Leone, Yoruba people from Nigeria and Limba people from Sierra Leone. However, his parents, Carolyn and Leroy Boseman are both African American (born in the U.S.A.). Chadwick's mother was a nurse. Chadwick saw his father work a lot of third shifts, a lot of night shifts; he worked at a textile factory, and also had a side business as an upholsterer. Chadwick has stated that "Whenever I work a particularly hard week, I think of him."

Chadwick was the youngest of three boys, who were raised as Christians. He was baptized, and was part of a church choir and youth group at the Welfare Baptist Church. His closest role models were his two brothers: Derrick, the eldest, now a preacher in Tennessee; and Kevin in the middle, a dancer who has performed with the Martha Graham and Alvin Ailey troupes and toured with the stage adaptation of "The Lion King."

Both brothers, each five years apart from the next, were allies and rivals. Chadwick always wanted to beat Derrick in sports. And he wanted to dress better than Kevin, who ultimately foreshadowed Chadwick's life in the arts. He had always insisted that he had something and was going to do it anyway, right or wrong, and as Chadwick said, "He was right."

Kevin had the resolve, and despite the odds, he persisted in his chosen career and ultimately, excelled. In Anderson in the 1980s there was little context for a boy who dreamed of becoming a dancer, let alone a black one, and it wasn't something that his family understood. However, in time, they came around, helping Kevin get into the Governor's School for the Arts and Humanities in nearby Greenville.

Some days, Chadwick's mother would take him with her to pick up his brother Kevin from school theater or dance rehearsals. Chadwick would watch the action onstage, mesmerized by verbal directions, which he strained to understand, and by the lights; and he became awed by the excitement of show business.

Chadwick attended T. L. Hanna High School, located outside the Anderson city limits at 2600 Highway 81 North. Anderson is a city in, and the county seat of, Anderson County, South Carolina, United States. At the census of 2000, there were 25,514 people, 10,641 households, and 6,299 families residing in the city. The population density was 1,843.7 people per square mile. There were 12,068 housing units at an average density of 872.1 per square mile. The racial makeup of the city was 63.12% White, 34.01% African American, 0.22% Native American, 0.78% Asian American, 0.04% Pacific Islander, 0.68% from other races, and 1.16% from two or more races. Hispanic or Latino of any race were 1.48% of the population.

Anderson became one of the first cities in the Southeastern United States to have electricity, which was established by William C. Whitner in 1895 at a hydroelectric plant on the Rocky River, giving the city the name "The Electric City." It also became the first city in the world to supply a cotton gin by electricity. Anderson is known as "The Friendliest City in South Carolina" and because of Its spirit and quality of life Anderson County earned national recognition being named an "All-America City" in 2000.

T.L. Hanna was Anderson School District 5's all-white high school (Westside was the African-American school). T.L. Hanna High gained national notoriety when James "Radio" Kennedy's story was made into a movie, in which **Radio** was portrayed by **Cuba Gooding Jr.** Radio was a young man with an intellectual disability who befriended T. L. Hanna Coach Harold Jones in 1964. Although Radio was not a student at Hanna, he and the coach became great friends, and Radio became a legend in Anderson.

In 1971, the district was integrated, nearly 20 years after the Supreme Court's 1954 ruling in Brown v. Board of Education. In 1989, T. L. Hanna High School was named "Palmetto's Finest" by the **South Carolina** Department of Education. In 1992, the school moved to its current location on Highway 81.

In high school, Chadwick was a serious basketball player but made a final turn toward storytelling after a friend and teammate was tragically shot and killed. Chadwick processed his thoughts and emotions; and in 1991, while in his junior year, his passion for acting and directing was realized. After the tragedy, he wrote and staged his first play, *Crossroads*, at their school. Chadwick graduated from T.L. Hanna High school in 1995.

Having been inspired by his brother Kevin's career in entertainment, Chadwick stated, "There's no way in the world I would have thought, 'O.K. let me write this play', if it wasn't for him. Ultimately, I'm here because of what Kevin did." When it was time to consider colleges, Chadwick chose an arts program at Howard University, with a dream of becoming a director.

In 2000, T.L. Hanna High was named a National Blue Ribbon School by the **U.S. Department of Education**. In 2014, *U.S. News & World Report* named T.L. Hanna as the fifth best high school in South Carolina and ranked it in the top 3% of high schools in the United States.

All in all, the small town school had some pretty notable alumni, including: **Chadwick Boseman**, actor, writer, and director, *Marshall, 42, Get On Up, Draft Day, Captain America: Civil War, Black Panther*; **James Michael Tyler**, actor who played Gunther on the sitcom "Friends"; **Martavis Bryant**, wide receiver for Oakland Raiders of NFL; **Jim Rice**, Baseball Hall of Fame player for **Boston Red Sox**, who attended his final year of high school there in 1971; and **Stephen D. Thorne**, NASA astronaut.

CHAPTER 2

EDUCATION COMES FIRST

Chadwick Boseman's success did not come overnight. He put many years into studying and honing his craft. After high school, he attended college at Howard University in Washington, DC, a historically black higher institution of learning.

Since 1867, Howard University has awarded more than 120,000 degrees in the professions, arts, sciences and humanities. Howard ranks among the highest producers of the nation's Black professionals in medicine, dentistry, pharmacy, engineering, nursing, architecture, religion, law, music, social work and education.

Regarded as one of the most prestigious institutions of higher learning in the world, Howard University's current enrollment approximates 11,000 students from virtually every state, the District of Columbia, and more than 70 countries. The University traditionally has had the largest gathering of Black scholars in the world.

When Chadwick Boseman enrolled at Howard University, he had initially planned to be just a writer and director. Chadwick graduated from Howard University in 2000 with a Bachelor of Fine Arts in directing.

He only studied acting to learn how to relate better with actors. But, apparently all that changed when he took an acting class presented by the Tony Award-winning actress and director Phylicia Rashad, who also became his mentor.

A native of Houston, Texas, Phylicia Rashad graduated Magna Cum Laude from Howard University.

Respected in the academic world, Rashad became the first recipient of the Denzel Washington Chair in Theatre at Fordham University. She received an Honorary Doctorate from Spelman College the year First Lady Michelle Obama delivered the 2011 commencement address. Ms. Rashad conducted Master Classes at the prestigious Ten Chimneys Foundation for the 2015 Lunt Fontanne Fellows. She also holds Honorary Doctorates from Fordham University, Carnegie Mellon University, Howard University, Providence College, Morris Brown College, Clark Atlanta University, Barber Scotia College, St. Augustine College, and Brown University.

A versatile performer, Rashad became a household name when she portrayed "Claire Huxtable" on *The Cosby Show*, a character whose appeal has earned her numerous honors and awards for over two decades. She later had a recurring role as "Diana

Dubois" on the popular Fox TV series *Empire* and is slated to appear in the upcoming Amazon series, *Jean Claude Van Johnson*.

While television was a catalyst in the rise of Rashad's career, she has also been a force on the stage, appearing both on and off-Broadway, often in projects that showcase her musical talent such as *Jelly's Last Jam, Into the Woods, Dreamgirls*, and *The Wiz*.

Inducted into the Theater Hall of Fame in 2016, Ms. Rashad received the 2016 Lucille Lortel Award for Outstanding Leading Actress in a Play for her performance as "Shelah" in Tarell Alvin McCraney's *Head of Passes* at the Public Theater.

She has performed on Broadway as "Violet Weston" in *August Osage County*, "Big Mama" in Tennessee Williams' *Cat on a Hot Tin Roof* (a role that she reprised on the London Stage), "Aunt Ester" in August Wilson's *Gem Of The Ocean*, (Tony Award nomination) and "Queen Britannia" in Shakespeare's *Cymbeline* at Lincoln Center.

Ms. Rashad also received both the Drama Desk and the Tony Award for Best Actress in a Play for her riveting performance as "Lena Younger" in the Broadway revival of Lorraine Hansberry's *A Raisin in The Sun*. She appeared in Ryan Coogler's *Creed*, Tyler Perry's *Good Deeds*, and starred in Perry's highly acclaimed film version of Ntozake Shange's *For Colored Girls Who Have Considered Suicide When The Rainbow Is Enuf.*

In 2015, Ms. Rashad received the BET Honors Theatrical Arts Award, Chicago Shakespeare Theatre's Spirit of Shakespeare Award, and the Inaugural Legacy Award of the Ruben Santiago Hudson Fine Arts Learning Center. Among the other awards that decorate her walls and shelves are the 2014 Mosaic Woman Legend Award of *Diversity Woman* Magazine, the Texas Medal of Arts, the National Council of Negro Women's Dorothy L. Height Dreammaker Award, AFTRA's AMEE Award for Excellence in Entertainment, the Board of Directors of New York Women In Film and Television's Muse Award for Outstanding Vision and Achievement, Dallas Women In Film Topaz Award, Peoples' Choice Awards, several NAACP Image Awards, and the Pan African Film Festival's Lifetime Achievement Award.

Whether she is bringing laughter to millions of television viewers around the world, moving theatre-goers to tears, thrilling movie fans, offering new insights to students by teaching Master Classes at renowned learning institutions that include Howard University, Julliard, and Carnegie Mellon, serving on Boards of prestigious organizations, or breaking new ground as a director, Phylicia Rashad is one of the entertainment world's most extraordinary performing artists.

While he was studying with Phylicia Rashad, Chadwick and some of his classmates were accepted for an elite theater program, the Oxford Mid-Summer Program of the British American Drama Academy in London. However, they didn't have the necessary funding; but Phylicia pushed for the students and got some celebrity friends to pay for them to go.

After Chadwick finished up the program, he received a beneficiary letter and figured out who had paid for him to attend. He learned that Phylicia's friend, Denzell Washington, had been a major contributor to his funding. He wrote Washington a thank you letter, but never gave it to him, and never told anyone else about it.

More than 20 years later, at the ***Black Panther*** film premiere, the two met and Chadwick finally was able to express his gratitude to Denzel in person. Shortly after the film's premiere, when Chadwick was on The Tonight Show, he told Jimmy Fallon that he has "basically been holding this secret [his] whole career," because Chadwick didn't want Washington to feel like he owed him anything else. He said that he wanted to meet him in person before saying anything, but after 20 years he felt like it would be okay to reveal it to the world.

Chadwick also revealed on The Tonight Show that he finally got to meet Denzell at the New York premiere of Black Panther, which was an "amazing" experience. Chadwick told Jimmy Fallon that he thanked Denzell for paying for his Oxford experience over two decades ago. In response, Denzell replied in jest, "Oh, so that's why I'm here. You owe me money! I came to collect!"

CHAPTER 3

SHARING HIS TALENTS

When he returned to the US, after college, Chadwick Boseman moved to the Bedford-Stuyvesant neighborhood of Brooklyn, where he lived at the start of his career, during most of his 20s. He wanted to write and direct, and initially began to study acting in order to learn how to relate to actors. He spent his days in coffee shops — playing chess and writing plays to direct, some of which were influenced by hip-hop and Pan-African theology. Chadwick then attended and graduated from New York City's Digital Film Academy. He later worked as the drama instructor in the Schomburg Junior Scholars Program, housed at the Schomburg Center for Research in Black Culture in Harlem, New York.

During that time, Chadwick also got minor roles in different TV shows. He got his first television role in 2003, in an episode of

Third Watch and in the series *All My Children*. His early work also included episodes of the series *Law & Order, CSI: NY,* and *ER*. Chadwick has appeared in episodes of *Cold Case, Lie to Me, The Glades, Castle, Detroit 1-8-7, Justified,* and *Fringe*.

A dramatist as well as an actor, Chadwick also continued to write plays, with his script for *Deep Azure* performed at the Congo Square Theatre Company in Chicago in 2005. *Deep Azure* was nominated for a 2006 Joseph Jefferson Award for New Work.

The **Joseph Jefferson Award**, *more commonly known informally as the **Jeff Award**, is given for theatre arts in the Chicago area. Founded in 1968, the awards are named in tribute to actor Joseph Jefferson, a 19th-century American theater star who, as a child, was a player in Chicago's first theater company. Two types of awards are given: "Equity" for work done under an Actors' Equity Association contract, and "Non-Equity" for non-union work. Award recipients are determined by a secret ballot.*

In 2008 Chadwick moved to Los Angeles, the entertainment capital of the world, to solely pursue an acting career. It was a decision that paid off immediately and he has not looked back since. Shortly after arriving in Los Angeles, Chadwick landed an acting job. He played a recurring role on the television series

Lincoln Heights and appeared in his first feature film, *The Express* as Floyd Little. In 2008 he won a Jury Award for Honorable Mention at the Hollywood Black Film Festival. He landed a regular role in 2010 in another television series, *Persons Unknown*.

After a couple of stagnant years in Los Angeles, Chadwick Boseman returned to New York where he directed an off-Broadway play in East Village. At the time, he was considering giving up acting and pursuing directing full-time. Then, his career took off by leaps and bounds. Chadwick's breakthrough role came in 2013 when he auditioned for the movie 42, which was a biopic for baseball pioneer, Jackie Robinson, who was the first African American to play in the major leagues in the 20th century. Robinson played for the Brooklyn Dodgers from 1947 until he retired in 1956. He played in 6 World Series and was a highly acclaimed baseball player. About 25 other actors had been seriously considered for the role, but director **Brian Helgeland** liked Chadwick's bravery and cast him after he had auditioned twice. Chadwick's performance in the movie got him named the "Male Star of Tomorrow" by the National Association of Theater Owners in 2014.

In 2013, Chadwick Boseman had also starred in the indie film *The Kill Hole*, which was released in theaters a few weeks before *42*. Suddenly, after ten years in the business, Chadwick was on fire. In addition, prior to their open casting, Universal selected Chadwick Boseman on August 26, 2013 to play the lead role in another high-profile project, *Get On Up*, a movie portraying the personal struggles and successes of music legend James Brown. Chadwick did all of his own dancing and some singing. The soundtrack is a live recording of James Brown music.

Then, on September 17, 2013 Universal announced an open casting call for actors, musicians, and extras for different roles in the biopic. The auditions were held on September 21st, almost a month after Chadwick had been selected. *Get on Up* was met with positive reviews from critics, with praise mainly going to Chadwick Boseman's performance. The film had a rating of 80% on the review aggregator site *Rotten Tomatoes*, based on 158 reviews, with an average rating of 6.9/10. The site's consensus reads: "With an unforgettable Chadwick Boseman in the starring role, *Get on Up* offers the "Godfather of Soul" a fittingly dynamic homage. *Get On Up* does justice to his unknowable soul and James Brown's unending music, both of which defy closure by definition."

Chadwick Bosman was on a roll and he has not missed a beat since. In 2014, Boseman appeared opposite **Kevin Costner** in *Draft Day*, in which he played an **NFL draft** prospect, Vontae Mack. Later that year, *Get on Up* was released in which he starred as **James Brown**. In 2016, Boseman came back with a vengeance when he starred as **Thoth**, a deity from Egyptian mythology, in *Gods of Egypt*.

Chadwick's former pastor said that he still keeps his faith. Chadwick has stated that he prayed to be the Black Panther *before* he was cast as the character in the **Marvel Cinematic Universe**. Chadwick's prayers were answered when he actually started portraying the **Marvel Comics** character T'Challa / Black Panther in 2016, with the blockbuster *Captain America: Civil War* being his first film in a five-picture deal with **Marvel**.

In 2017, Chadwick briefly returned to biographical movies with *Marshall*, where he played Thurgood Marshall. Thurgood Marshall was an extraordinary Civil Rights attorney who won hundreds of cases, including the Brown VS Brown which desegregated all white schools throughout America so that African American students could attend high schools with white children. He became the first African American Supreme Court Justice. President Lyndon Johnson nominated him to be the first

African American Supreme Court Justice. Thurgood Marshall sat on the United States Supreme Court from October 1967 until October 1991. He died in 1993.

After *Marshall*, Chadwick continued his role as Black Panther. He headlined the Academy Award nominated *Black Panther*, which focused on Boseman's character as the King of Wakanda, who is also the Black Panther and his home country of Wakanda in Africa. The movie was released in February 2018 to rave reviews, becoming one of the highest-grossing films of the year in the United States. Black Panther shattered box office records by raking in an estimated $218 million in the United States alone over the four-day President's Day weekend.

In April 2018, Boseman rejoined his other Marvel cohorts; Capt. America, Iron Man, etc. in the movie *Avengers: Infinity War*. He returned in *Avengers: Endgame*, which was released in April 2019.

CHAPTER 4

AVENGERS ENDGAME

*A*vengers: Endgame is a 2019 American superhero film, based on the Marvel Comics superhero team the Avengers, produced by Marvel Studios and distributed by Walt Disney Studios Motion Pictures. It is the sequel to 2012's *The Avengers*, 2015's *Avengers: Age of Ultron*, and 2018's *Avengers: Infinity War*, and the twenty-second film in the Marvel Cinematic Universe (MCU). It was directed by Anthony and Joe Russo and written by Christopher Markus and Stephen McFeely, and features an ensemble cast including Robert Downey Jr., Chris Evans, Mark Ruffalo, Chris Hemsworth, Scarlett Johansson, Jeremy Renner, Don Cheadle, Paul Rudd, Brie Larson, Karen Gillan, Danai Gurira, Benedict Wong, Jon Favreau, Bradley Cooper, Gwyneth Paltrow, and Josh Brolin.

Several actors from *Infinity War* reprised their roles in *Endgame,* including **Chadwick Boseman as T'Challa / Black Panther**. In the film, the surviving members of the Avengers and their allies attempt to reverse the damage caused by Thanos in *Infinity War*.

Twenty-three days after Thanos used the Infinity Gauntlet to disintegrate half of all life in the universe, Carol Danvers rescues Tony Stark and Nebula from deep space and returns them to Earth, where they reunite with the remaining Avengers—Bruce Banner, Steve Rogers, Thor, Natasha Romanoff, and James Rhodes—and Rocket. Locating Thanos on an otherwise uninhabited planet, they plan to retake and use the Infinity Stones to reverse "the Snap", but Thanos reveals he destroyed the Stones to prevent their further use. Enraged, Thor decapitates Thanos.

Five years later, Scott Lang escapes from the quantum realm. At the Avengers compound, he explains to Romanoff and Rogers that he experienced only five hours while trapped. Theorizing the quantum realm could allow time travel, the three ask Stark to help them retrieve the Stones from the past to reverse Thanos' actions in the present. Stark refuses, thinking of his wife, Pepper Potts, and daughter, Morgan, but relents after looking at a picture of himself and Peter Parker. Stark and Banner, who has since merged his intelligence with the Hulk's strength, build a time machine. Banner notes that changing the past does not affect their present; any changes instead create branched alternate realities. He and Rocket visit the Asgardian refugees' new home in Norway—New Asgard—to recruit Thor, now overweight and drinking heavily, despondent over his failure to stop Thanos. In Tokyo, Romanoff recruits Clint Barton, now a vigilante subsequent to the disintegration of his family.

Banner, Lang, Rogers, and Stark travel to New York City in 2012. Banner visits the Sanctum Sanctorum and convinces the Ancient One to give him the Time Stone. At Stark Tower, Rogers retrieves the Mind Stone, but Stark and Lang's attempt to steal the Space Stone fails, allowing 2012 Loki to escape with it. Rogers and Stark travel to S.H.I.E.L.D. headquarters in 1970, where Stark obtains an earlier version of the Space Stone and encounters his father, Howard, while Rogers steals Pym Particles from Hank Pym to return to the present. Meanwhile, Rocket and Thor travel to Asgard in 2013, extracting the Reality Stone from Jane Foster and retrieving Thor's hammer, Mjolnir. Nebula and Rhodes travel to Morag in 2014 and steal the Power Stone before Peter Quill can. Rhodes returns to the present with the Power Stone, but Nebula becomes incapacitated when her cybernetic implants link with those of her past self. Through this connection, 2014 Thanos learns of his future success and the Avengers' attempts to undo it. He captures Nebula and sends 2014 Nebula to the present in the former's place. Barton and Romanoff travel to Vormir in 2014, where the Soul Stone's keeper, the Red Skull, reveals it can only be acquired by sacrificing someone they love. Romanoff sacrifices herself, allowing Barton to obtain the Soul Stone.

Reuniting in the present, the Avengers place the Stones into a Stark-created gauntlet, which Banner, the most resistant to the Stones' gamma radiation, uses to reverse the disintegrations. Meanwhile, 2014 Nebula uses the time machine to transport 2014 Thanos and his warship to the present, where he attacks the Avengers' compound, planning to destroy and rebuild the universe with the Stones. Nebula convinces 2014 Gamora to betray Thanos but fails to convince 2014 Nebula and is forced to kill her. Confronted by Stark, Thor, and a Mjolnir-wielding Rogers, Thanos outmatches them and summons his army from his warship to devastate Earth. **Stephen Strange**, restored to life, arrives and brings other sorcerers, the restored Avengers and Guardians of the Galaxy, the Ravagers, and the **armies of Wakanda** and Asgard to fight Thanos and his army, alongside Danvers, who destroys Thanos' warship as she arrives. After overpowering the heroes, Thanos seizes the gauntlet, but Stark steals the Stones back and uses them to disintegrate Thanos and his army, at the cost of his life.

Following Stark's funeral, Thor appoints Valkyrie as the new ruler of New Asgard and joins the Guardians of the Galaxy. Rogers returns the Infinity Stones and Mjolnir to their original timelines and remains in the past to live with Peggy Carter. In the present, an elderly Rogers passes his shield and mantle on to Sam Wilson.

The film was announced in October 2014 as *Avengers: Infinity War – Part 2*. The Russo brothers came on board to direct in April 2015, and by May, Markus and McFeely signed on to write the script for the film. In July 2016, Marvel removed the film's title, and it remained untitled until its official title was revealed in December 2018. Filming began in August 2017 at Pinewood Atlanta Studios in Fayette County, Georgia, shooting back-to-back with *Infinity War*, and ended in January 2018. Additional filming took place in the Metro and Downtown Atlanta areas, New York, Scotland and England. With an estimated budget of $356 million, it is one of the most expensive films ever made.

Avengers: Endgame was widely anticipated, and Disney backed the film with extensive marketing campaigns. It premiered in Los Angeles on April 22, 2019, and was theatrically released in the United States on April 26, 2019, in IMAX and 3D. The film received praise for its direction, acting, musical score, action sequences, visual effects, and emotional weight, with critics lauding its culmination of the 22-film story. It grossed nearly $2.8 billion worldwide, surpassing *Infinity War*'s entire theatrical run in just eleven days and breaking numerous box office records, including becoming the highest-grossing film of all time, overtaking 2009's *Avatar*.

CHADWICK'S PHOTO JOURNEY

Chadwick portrayed as Marvel's Messiah in Rolling Stone photoshoot

Getting Ready for Action

The Unforgettable Four

Black Panther Leading Ladies

Presenting at the Golden Globes wearing Verace

Looking Regal at the 2018 Met Gala

Closeup at the 2018 Met Gala

Wakanda Forever

Chadwick on the Tonight Show with Jimmy Fallon

Chadwick & Taylor at the 2019 Sag Awards

Black Panther Cast accepting award for Outstanding Motion Picture at 50th Annual NAACP Image Awards

*Chadwick and Lupita congratulating each
other at the 25th Annual Screen Actors Guild Awards*

(L-R) Sterling K. Brown, winner of Outstanding Performance by a Cast in a Motion Picture for 'Black Panther' and Outstanding Performance by an Ensemble in a Drama Series for 'This Is Us;' Angela Bassett, Lupita Nyong'o, Chadwick Boseman, Danai Gurira, Michael B. Jordan, and Andy Serkis, winners of Outstanding Performance by a Cast in a Motion Picture for 'Black Panther,' pose in the press room during the 25th Annual Screen Actors Guild Awards at The Shrine Auditorium on January 27, 2019 in Los Angeles, California.

Marvel Studios made the entire world shout "Wakanda Forever!" when Black Panther *hit theaters in February 2018, kicking off a spectacular run that has made the film one of the* highest-grossing movies of all time, worldwide, *with the best reviews of* any movie in Marvel's cinematic universe. *So, of course, Disney is making a sequel.*

CHAPTER 5

WAKANDA FOREVER! BLACK PANTHER 2

With the box office successes of *Infinity War, Endgame* and *Black Panther 1, Black Panther 2* is inevitable, at this point. And Marvel has promised a number of sequels and spin-offs. Black Panther has become one of the biggest movies in the Marvel Cinematic Universe. It now holds the record for biggest February debut and has gone on to have the second-highest second weekend in box office history. Ryan Coogler, the director, has dropped a cultural phenomenon in theaters; and moviegoers, who wouldn't normally go see superhero movies, are going in droves to see Chadwick Boseman's T'Challa and Wakanda on the big screen.

The return of Chadwick Boseman as T'Challa in ***Black Panther 2*** is also inevitable at this point in time. Movies that do this well always end up with sequels. Plus, producer Nate Moore already confirmed the possibility of multiple sequels only weeks into production of the first adventure.

There is no longer a need to speculate. Here's everything you need to know about *Black Panther 2* so far.

- **Title:** *Black Panther 2* (working title)

- **Release date**: May 6, 2022

- **Cast**: Chadwick Boseman, Lupita Nyong'o, Danai Gurira, Letitia Wright, Winston Duke, Daniel Kaluuya

- **Director**: Ryan Coogler

Yes! Nearly all of the cast of *Black Panther* are expected to return for the sequel, with Chadwick Boseman's T'Challa leading an ensemble that also includes Wakandan characters portrayed by Lupita Nyong'o (Nakia), Danai Gurira (Okoye), Letitia Wright

(Shuri), Winston Duke (M'Baku), and Daniel Kaluuya (W'Kabi). Martin Freeman is also expected to reprise his role as CIA agent Everett K. Ross. It has also been indicated that *Black Panther* actor **Michael B. Jordan** might also reprise his role — in some form, at least — as Erik Killmonger in the follow-up film.

Black Panther, released in February 2018, was a groundbreaking entry in the Marvel Cinematic Universe with the box office gross and cultural impact to prove it. It was also one of the last movies to be released in Marvel's Phase Three, hitting theaters just before *Avengers: Infinity War*, which set the stage for *Avengers: Endgame* April 2019.

King T'Challa, aka the Black Panther himself, had made his debut in *Captain America: Civil War*, starred in his solo film, and then was promptly turned to dust at the end of *Infinity War*. On this side of *Endgame*, he's back. But what does the future hold for him? Here's everything we know about **Black Panther 2**, including new details about the plot, casting information, who's directing, and more.

Marvel head honcho, Kevin Feige, had already expressed his desire to bring back director Ryan Coogler to do the sequel. Feige brought up his wish for Coogler to return for **Black Panther 2** before the first movie had even hit theaters. Marvel has made it a habit to stick with certain directors, which makes the return of Coogler almost 100 percent, at this point. Plus, the director expressed his enthusiasm for working with Marvel a number of times, so we know that the working relationship is there behind-the-scenes. In October 2018, *The Hollywood Reporter* announced that **Ryan Coogler will be back** to direct the *Black Panther* sequel. According to *THR*'s report, Coogler has already begun working on the script (as of April 2019). Marvel Studios publicly confirmed Coogler's involvement, August 2019, during Disney's D23 convention.

Confirmed to **return as the writer and director** on *Black Panther 2*, Ryan Coogler indicated that he's well aware of the unique pressure on him to replicate the success of the first film. "I've had a chance to make three feature films, each one of them had its own very specific type of pressure. In the process of it, it feels insurmountable each time," Coogler told **IndieWire**. "When it comes to making a sequel, I've never done it before — a sequel to something that I've directed myself. So, I think there's going to be a lot of pressure there, but what we're going to try to do is just focus on the work, like we always do. [We'll] really try to go step by step and try to quiet everything else around us, really focus on trying to make something that has some type of meaning."

*Ryan Coogler with Marvel Studios President Kevin Feige
at Disney's 2019 D23 convention.*

When Is Black Panther 2's Release Date?

Black Panther 2 will be the first movie in Marvel Studios' Phase Five after *Thor: Love and Thunder* closes out Phase Four. At Disney's 2019 D23 convention, Marvel Studios President Kevin Feige called writer-director Ryan Coogler out on stage to confirm a May 6, 2022 release date for the film.

Who Is Starring in *Black Panther 2*?

Chadwick Boseman will reprise his role as T'Challa, having been revived by the Hulk during *Avengers: Endgame*. It's similarly a safe bet that Letitia Wright will be back as Shuri, Lupita Nyong'o will return as Nakia, and Danai Gurira will return to play Okoye.

Chadwick Boseman and Letitia Wright in 'Black Panther'

Danai Gurira and Florence Kasumba in 'Black Panther'

Winston Duke will also likely return for *Black Panther 2* as M'Baku, who is now more ready than ever to team up with T'Challa to protect Wakanda after the events of the first *Black Panther, Infinity War*, and *Endgame*. Additional likely returning cast members include Daniel Kaluuya (as W'Kabi) and Angela Bassett (as Queen Mother Ramonda).

Martin Freeman, who played CIA agent Everett Ross, **confirmed to** *Collider* that he will return to the MCU and likely in the sequel to *Black Panther*, but admitted he didn't know much. "As far as I know, I will be in another *Black Panther*. That's my understanding. As to when that will happen, I don't know," he said.

What Is the Plot of *Black Panther 2*?

No plot details about *Black Panther 2* are known at this time, but after *Endgame*, we can make some major guesses.

Black Panther 2 will have to address the events of *Avengers: Infinity War* and *Endgame*, especially since much of the action in the former film happened in T'Challa's home nation of Wakanda. T'Challa and Shuri both died in Thanos' Decimation, so the Wakandan leadership must have struggled for the five-year gap between *Infinity War* and *Endgame*.

When we see T'Challa and Shuri at the end of *Endgame*, they're standing on a balcony at the palace, looking out at Wakanda with their mother. But the politics won't be so simple by *Black Panther 2*, right? It is possible that the movie could ignore

Endgame altogether and essentially fast-forward to some other conflict in real-time.

We can expect the world of *Black Panther* to expand and move forward, regardless. The end of the first film saw T'Challa opening the borders of Wakanda, ending a long chapter in the nation's history as an isolated country. This will inevitably factor into the sequel and it could mean new characters will be introduced, as well as a more global story.

Who Is the Villain in *Black Panther 2*?

The villain of the *Black Panther* sequel is still unknown.

In May 2018, <u>*Metro UK*</u> reported that Michael B. Jordan might reprise his role as Killmonger, but that seems suspicious given his death in *Black Panther*. Perhaps he might pop up in the mystical afterlife that the Black Panther visits to speak with his ancestors?

Michael B. Jordan and Chadwick Boseman in 'Black Panther'

Michael B. Jordan and Chadwick Boseman in 'Black Panther'

It's also rumored Donald Glover might be involved with *Black Panther 2*. According to the same *Metro* report, Glover has apparently been in talks with Coogler to play a new character who may or may not be a villain. Glover already has a role in the MCU as Aaron Davis. In the comics, Aaron is the uncle of Peter

Parker's Spider-Man successor, Miles Morales, and a criminal who suits up as the villain Prowler.

Furthermore, *Endgame* may have provided a clue: During a confab between Natasha, Okoye, Rhodey, Carol Danvers, Nebula, and Rocket, Okoye mentions that there have been underwater earthquakes detected under Wakanda. At the time, Okoye seems ready to brush it off, but it seems to get Black Widow's attention and it turns into a talking point during the meeting. But when Okoye assures Natasha that they're handling it, the issue is never addressed again.

Is this Marvel hinting at **Namor**? While the character's film rights may or may not be tied up with Universal Studios, Marvel may have arranged **a similar arrangement to the Hulk** to use Namor in the MCU without producing a solo Namor film. Marvel Studios' schedule is already packed with films like *Black Widow*, *The Eternals*, *Doctor Strange in the Multiverse of Madness*, and *Thor: Love and Thunder*, leaving no room for Black Panther in 2020 or 2021. *Black Panther 2* — which isn't the official title — will drop on May 6, 2022, kicking off the summer blockbuster season. Marvel hasn't said if *Black Panther 2* is officially considered part of Phase 4 of the MCU, or if it will join *Blade* and others as part of Phase 5.

Chadwick Boseman is T'Challa, aka Black Panther. The actor has graced the covers of Time and Rolling Stone Magazine, gaining high praise for his performance in the first installment. He is believed to have signed a 5-movie contract to Marvel Studios for the role. Chadwick studied African personalities like Nelson Mandela and Fela Kuti and he also traveled to South Africa twice, where the fictional country's accent is based.

Boseman is a must for **Black Panther 2** after making his debut in *Captain America: Civil War* and wowing audiences before they even knew that a Black Panther movie was being planned. It's important to mention that we still do not know who makes it out of *Infinity War* and *Avengers 4* alive, at this point; but it's safe to say that Lupita Nyong'o's Nakia is fairly safe, along with Letitia Wright's Shuri. Shuri may end up as the new Tony Stark in the next phase of the MCU, which makes her very important and almost guaranteed that she'll make it through the bloody battle with Thanos and his Black Order. Martin Freeman's Everett Ross could also make an appearance since the actor has confirmed that the character will be in future MCU projects.

It's safe to say that Michael B. Jordan's Erik Killmonger will not be making a return in **Black Panther 2**, unless it's through flashbacks. The Black Panther character has been around for decades and there are a lot of villains to choose from. Ryan

Coogler admitted that he originally wanted to bring in Kraven the Hunter for the first movie, but Marvel did not have the rights. However, now that the first movie was such a hit, we might be able to see Kraven the Hunter hit the big screen for the first time in **Black Panther 2**. M'Baku could also make a return as Man Ape (though they don't call him this in the movie), since he is left alive and well after the events of the first installment. Nakia actually becomes a villain in the comics, so there's that possibility, as well. Baron Zemo, King Cadaver, Achebe, Namor: The Sub-Mariner, and Klaw are also heavy contenders.

The MCU will look a lot different than it looks now after the events of *Infinity War* and *Avengers 4*. We're still not sure what characters will make it out alive from the massive battle with the villainous Thanos and his Black Order. Whatever happens in the aftermath of those two movies will set the tone for the new phase of the MCU. We know that *Guardians of the Galaxy Vol. 3* is on the way as is *Captain Marvel*, which makes one think that some of those characters could end up in Wakanda for **Black Panther 2** or we could see Chadwick Boseman's T'Challa in another location. The end of the first movie suggests that Wakanda will offer up its precious Vibranium to the world, so that could be another factor. Additionally, if the Disney and Fox deal goes through, we could see the marriage between T'Challa and the *X-Men*'s Storm. There's a lot of ways that **Black Panther 2** can play out and it will be interesting to see where the MCU takes the Black Panther franchise.

While Storm has not been brought up by Ryan Coogler, he has said that Marvel boss Kevin Feige is the right man to bring the X-Men to the MCU. **Black Panther 2** will come out after the final decision is made for the Disney and Fox deal, so it is possible that the *X-Men* will be back to Marvel by that time. T'Challa and Storm had a romance in the comic series and were even married for a short time. The two were divorced during the events of the *Avengers* vs. *X-Men* event in 2012. When asked about the possibility of the romance, Chadwick Boseman joked, "Are you trying to break up my relationship with Nakia? It sounds like that's what you're doing right now."

Black Panther was first introduced in *Captain America: Civil War*. Wakanda and T'Challa were a significant portion of *Infinity War* and *Avengers 4*. So, there's at least two places that we have seen Black Panther and Wakanda on the big screen before the events of **Black Panther 2**. It seems highly unlikely that he'll make a cameo in *Ant-Man and the Wasp* or *Captain Marvel*, but Wakanda will more than likely be mentioned, especially since the world now knows about Vibranium. However, Martin Freeman's Everett Ross has been rumored to show up in *Captain Marvel* since it takes place in the early 1990s, which is when he was in the Air Force.

Letitia Wright's Shuri character was in *Infinity War* and she may be the new Tony Stark genius of the group. Fans were glad to see her interact with Stark and Bruce Banner to see who the biggest nerd of the group is. Additionally, Angela Basset's Queen Mother Ramonda showed up in *Infinity War* as well along with T'Challa's most trusted general and ally, Okoye, played by Danai Gurira. It seems likely that we'll see the return of Winston Duke's M'Baku, since he later became an ally at the end of the first movie.

A hardcore Black Panther fan recently started a petition to have Marvel develop a TV series that chronicles the history of Wakanda. The petition wants the show to be set up on Netflix, but if something like this moves forward, it will be through Disney's own streaming service. It would be pretty cool to see the history of Wakanda unfold and see how they became the most technologically advanced country on the planet, how this remained a secret for all of these years, and how they came to utilize their Vibranium. A mini-series would be a great way to promote the upcoming ***Black Panther 2***, so that could very well happen.

It seems logical that we would get our first look at the movie around 6 to 8 months before the premiere. The first trailer for Black Panther made its debut in June of 2017, which was pretty far in advance of the February 2018 release date. If the marketing campaign follows the same patterns, we can expect to see a TV spot first and then have an official full-length trailer drop at some point afterwards with a few different TV spots. Black Panther did a great job of teasing footage without giving much away and even had an epic Super Bowl commercial in 2018. One thing is for certain, everything will be ramped up considerably after the success of the first movie. So, in all likelihood, the first footage we see from ***Black Panther 2*** won't strike until 2021 at the earliest.

Since the official release date has been set for 2022 for ***Black Panther 2***, a specific date to buy tickets is not currently set. However, pre-sale tickets for the first movie went on sale about 5 weeks before the premiere, which seems to be the tradition for the larger movies lately. Black Panther broke Fandango's record for the most Marvel Cinematic Universe pre-sale tickets sold. In addition, the movie broke the pre-sale records for the month of February in box office history, so when pre-sale tickets go on sale for ***Black Panther 2***, you can bet that they'll be hard to get.

CHAPTER 6

MORE ABOUT CHADWICK BOSEMAN

His Politics

Boseman was thrust into a media spotlight when cast as Black Panther, a king of a fictional nation in Africa. The very casting gave reporters the opening to ask Boseman about his feelings about politics.

Surprisingly, his answer came before the release of *Black Panther* when Boseman did the press rounds for *Marshall* in fall 2017. "First of all, I'm not just an actor, I'm an artist," the actor told the press. "You have to express the full scope of your being, physically, spiritually, and that includes politically, which includes Donald Trump's presidency." Chadwick then offered the opinion that "if Trump can't take the criticism from the people, don't be the president."

His Religion

Boseman was raised Christian and, according to his former pastor, remains a part of the faith. "He did a lot of positive things within the church and within the community," said Pastor Samuel Neely from the Welfare Baptist Church (located at 2106 Bolt Dr, Belton, SC 29627). "With him singing in the choir, with him working with the youth group, he always was doing something, always helping out, always serving. That was his personality."

Chadwick Boseman's family has a longtime history as members of the Welfare Baptist Church, which had its beginnings in 1867, only five years after President Abraham Lincoln signed the Emancipation Proclamation. Like many historically African American congregations, its organization came out of a predominantly white congregation, Neals Creek Baptist Church. By the help of our Lord and Savior, the freeing of those who had worshipped under the fig trees of their masters had finally become a reality.

On September 5, 1867 thirty-three community leaders, including Catae Rice, Eli Greenlee, Samuel Geer, Ceasar Hammons, Milton Thompson, William Scott, Richmond Ellis, and Carolina Rice united themselves together to form a workable organization.

During this meeting, the group invited Reverend F. S. Morris, Reverend H. R. Vandiver, and Reverend J. C. Horton to officiate. After carefully examining the cause for a new congregation with doctrinal principles began as an independent Baptist church.

During the following months the first pastor, Reverend Phillip Morris of Anderson, South Carolina, was elected. At the same meeting the first deacons were also elected: Catae Rice, Eli Greenlee, and Milton Thompson.

On October 7, 1871, the church contacted Enoch Vandiver for the purchase of two acres of land, located between Belton and Anderson at a cost of $10.00. The amount of purchase was paid by a loyal member, William Scott.

Reverend Morris exhibited great leadership. Through his dedication and faithfulness of the members, the first building, a log cabin edifice, was built. Reverend Morris resigned in 1970 leaving a congregation exceeding 125 members.

Six pastors served from 1870 until 1890. Each pastor did his very best to teach, preach and lead the congregation to new challenges. In 1890, Reverend J. A. Pinson was elected the seventh pastor of Welfare. Under his tenure, a community leader, James N. Anderson, deeded three acres of land to the church. Like many other African American churches, a schoolhouse was built. Professor Redman was hired as the principal and teacher.

After setting up an effective program, Professor Redman resigned. The second teacher was Lena Watkins, the daughter of Dr. Harrison Watkins. Upon Mrs. Watkins decision to leave, Professor Redman returned as principal/teacher. Upon his resignation, Clara McCullough was elected principal to fill the position. Upon completion of her education, Ms. McCullough, now <u>Clara M. Boseman</u>, an early relative of Chadwick's, returned as teacher. <u>Mrs. Boseman</u> was an active member in the Welfare family.

In the early 1930s, a two-room schoolhouse was built. <u>Mrs. Boseman</u> served as principal/teacher and Emma Thompson was hired as a second teacher. These two ladies taught until the school was closed in the 1950s.

In 1901, Doctor Harrison Watkins returned to Welfare as its eleventh pastor. During the late twenties, Doctor Watkin's eyesight began to fail. Soon he became blind. Doctor Watkins died in 1932. Deacons ordained by Doctor Watkins were: Silas Jones, Michael Rice, Henry Dean, Andy Whitner, Henry Ellis, Perry Nance, Henry Peterson, Floyd Brown, Frank Brown,

Washington Reid, Franklin Kay, and <u>M. T. Boseman</u>, who was another early relative of Chadwick's.

In 1934, Reverend Homer Brown of Williamston, South Carolina was elected as pastor. Reverend Brown served for two years. He died in 1936.

In 1936, Revered L. E. Daniel of Belton, South Carolina succeeded Revered Brown. After accepting a position on the staff of Morris College, Reverend Daniel resigned in 1944.

In January 1945, Doctor H. W. D. Stewart of Greenville, South Carolina was elected the fourteenth pastor. Under his administration, the membership built its first brick building. The new building was tri-level, well lighted, and centrally heated. It was equipped with indoor facilities, a modern kitchen and many Sunday School rooms. The sanctuary was carpeted, and a new piano and organ were purchased. Doctor Stewart resigned in 1962. Deacons serving under Dr. Stewart were: William T. Agnew, W. L. Scott, Joe C. Kay, Cecil Mattison, Ralph Rice, <u>James Boseman</u>, <u>Elliott Boseman, R. M. Boseman</u>, great uncles of Chadwick's, Sylvester Clinkscales, James Dean and Joe Brown.

In 1963, Doctor Moses Patterson Robertson of Pendleton, South Carolina was elected as the fifteenth pastor. Born in Fairfield County, South Carolina, Doctor Robertson successfully pastored several churches before coming to Welfare. Under his leadership the church was renovated with a number of interior and exterior changes. In addition to the renovation, the church witnessed the revitalizing of its program. The following groups were organized: Finance Committee, Trustee Board, Pulpit Aid Auxiliary, Boy Scouts, Young Men's Progressive Club, Men's Chorus, the Inspirational Choir, Young People's Choir, and Children's Choir of which young Chadwick was a member.

On October 2, 1984, Doctor Robertson retired as pastor. Deacons ordained under Doctor Robertson were: W. A. Bolden, Roger Boseman, an uncle of Chadwick's, A. C. Ellis, Clyde Evans, Mack Nance, William Hunter and Charles Smith. Transferred to Welfare were Deacons Donnie Gambrell, Sr. (New Hopewell), and Jone Blanding (Evergreen).

On Tuesday, June 25, 1985, a call meeting by the Board of Deacons, Reverend Samuel Bernard Neely, Sr. was elected the sixteenth pastor. Reverend Neely, a native of Fountain Inn, South Carolina was, at the time of his election living In Mauldin,

South Carolina and was pastoring the Mount Zion Baptist Church in Laurens, South Carolina.

Rev. Neely's accomplishments have been many. Under his leadership the remaining mortgage of $86,000.00 was liquidated. The mortgage burning service was held on third Sunday in November 1988. On January 1, 1987, he became the first fulltime pastor of the church. In August of 1987, the existing sanctuary was renovated. In August 1990, 40 acres of land were purchased at a total of $115,000.00. This addition gave the church a total of 56 acres.

Other than physical improvements, the church grew in its attendance and spiritually. The youth department held its first youth camp during the summer of 1986. The youth held its first retreat on Hilton Head Island in July 1990. The youth department, in which <u>Chadwick Boseman</u> had been a member, was reorganized in 1990 to have its monthly youth services in the old sanctuary. The Young Men's Brotherhood was revitalized in 1986. In 1992, a special anti-drug support program was organized, Life Support Services.

The following deacons were ordained under Doctor Neely's administration: Maxie O. Agnew, Sr., <u>J. T. Boseman</u>, a cousin of Chadwick's, Elijah Clemons, Frank Evans, Onice Gray, Jr., Calvin

Henry, Sr., Avery James, Jr., Raymond James, Rodney Jones, Willie Lee, Jr., Thomas Ligon, Moffett Martin, Gannie L. McDavid, Sherwin M. Rice, Charles Scott, Undrea Walker, James Ware, and Mahlon Willis. Doctor Neely retired as Pastor of Welfare Baptist Church, February 2015.

In the fall of 2016, Reverend Ankoma Anderson, Sr., of Greenwood, South Carolina, became the seventeenth pastor. His focus is: Welfare, a Church Serving Four Generations. In 2017 Welfare Baptist Church celebrated its 150th Church Anniversary.

His Inner Strength

Although Chadwick Boseman had played the leading role in several other biopic movies prior to this year, his dynamic portrayal of T'Challa, the superhero in Marvel's blockbuster 2018 release *Black Panther*, cemented his place in the Hollywood firmament.

But it seems it's no coincidence that Chadwick Boseman, who has portrayed iconic black male figures such as Jackie Robinson (*42*, 2013), James Brown (*Get on Up*, 2014), and Thurgood Marshall (*Thurgood*, 2017), possesses many of the same qualities of his onscreen characters. He told the *Times* he builds a kind of bridge to these larger-than-life roles through a process of normalizing his subjects to better understand them.

"His method of humanizing superhumans begins with searching their pasts. He's looking for gestational wounds, personal failures, private fears—fissures where the molten ore of experience might harden into steel," the *Times* writes.

Of course, it also doesn't hurt that the 41-year-old South Carolina native is blessed with chiseled, movie-star good looks and has developed a dogged work ethic and relentless hustle gained through years of scrambling for small roles and writing plays in the New York acting scene. All this paid off once he made the move to L.A.—within two years of switching coasts, he had landed the starring role in *42*.

In November 2019, with *21 Bridges*, a New York City police drama and *Expatriate*, a spy thriller and the sequel to *Black Panther* on the way, the world is finally getting to see the full A-list star wattage as well as off-screen intelligence and coolness of Chadwick Boseman.

What makes him the man who plays men who stand tall? Brian Helgeland, the writer and director of "42," the Jackie Robinson movie that gave Boseman his breakout role, said that the actor reminded him of sturdy, self-assured icons of 1970s virility, like Gene Hackman and Clint Eastwood.

"It's the way he carries himself, his stillness — you just have that feeling that you're around a strong person," Helgeland said. He remembered choosing Boseman to anchor his film after seeing only two other auditions. "There's a scene in the movie where Robinson's teammate, Pee Wee Reese, puts his arm around him as a kind of show of solidarity. But Chad flips it on its head. He plays it like, 'I'm doing fine, I'm tough as nails, but go ahead and put your arm around me if it makes you feel better.' I think that's who Chad is as a person."

Lupita Nyong'o, Boseman's co-star and love interest in "Black Panther," described his career choices as those of a socially conscious history buff. She recalled a working session with the film's director, Ryan Coogler, and Boseman that he turned into a mini lecture on the ancient Egyptian iconography and spiritual customs that had informed the original comic book.

"He's very keen to put human experiences in historical context," she said. "Even with a world that was make-believe, he wanted to connect it to the world that we know and could try to understand."

Chadwick said, "They can put the clothes on you," finally, after a long pause. A wry smile fanned across his face — both rows of teeth, steady eye contact. "But then you've gotta wear 'em."

Next up are starring roles in the New York police action drama "21 Bridges" (of which he is also a producer), the international thriller "Expatriate" (he's producing and co-writing that one) and, barring an alien-invasion-level catastrophe, a wildly anticipated "Black Panther" sequel.

Remarkably, Chadwick Boseman has come this far despite a relatively late start (he led a studio film for the first time at 35) and while remaining noticeably untouched by the tabloid drama, or whiff of overexposure, that can engulf even seasoned celebrities. In a pop taxonomy of black male nobility, he is cut squarely from the mold of Barack Obama — generally cool, affable, devoted to unglamorous fundamentals — a figure whom he is doubtlessly on a shortlist to portray in an inevitable epic.

For the role of T'Challa, a.k.a. Black Panther, that meant conceiving of a childhood squeezed by the weight of an ancient unbroken dynasty. When it came to becoming Jackie Robinson, he focused on formative years as a Negro League firebrand that crystallized the baseball pioneer's polished exterior. James Brown: a meditation on irrepressible self-confidence, long starved by years of deprivation and insult in Jim Crow South Carolina.

According to Chadwick, "You have to hold it all in your mind, scene by scene. You're a strong black man in a world that conflicts with that strength, that really doesn't want you to be great. So, what makes you the one who's going to stand tall?"

When he was booked for a recurring role in the 2007-9 ABC Family series "Lincoln Heights," which filmed in Los Angeles, it afforded Chadwick his first real taste of Hollywood, which he liked more than he'd expected. Before that, he had just wanted to be an artist in New York, not understanding that coming to L.A. and trying to be a film actor was a completely different thing. But he was a quick study. He realized that. *If you've got New York hustle In L.A., what is there to think about?*

His Views on Black Culture in the Mainstream

As the lead actor in a very prominent mainstream movie with a substantial black cast, Chadwick Boseman has been asked multiple times what his personal feelings are about representation in popular culture.

"Black History Month is extremely important because we actually do need to make people focus on black history at a particular time because it's not done in our education system," Chadwick said. "It's not done even sometimes in our churches. It's not done enough. I also feel like we just have a month where we do it. You know? It's my belief that it's something you should do all the time because black history is part of all of our history."

His Daily Workout Routine

Being an actor can be very demanding, mentally as well as physically. The physical part is most obvious because of the variables in the characters you are portraying. Most importantly for Chadwick, playing any superhero is difficult; but when you are playing King of Wakanda, a warrior and the richest superhero, you need to look your absolute best on screen. Fortunately for Chadwick, even though lately he is playing the role of a serious superhero, he does not need to be too serious about his diet. Due to his high metabolism, Chadwick always has a lean figure which usually fits with the body type of the characters that he portrays. Therefore, his diet is not restricted, however, his fitness routine is quite strenuous, but very effective in order to keep him toned and muscle-bound.

Chadwick Boseman works out 5 days per week:

On day one he practices gymnastics and core.

- He warms up with stretches, Pull-ups squats pushups and jogging of 800m.

- Then the intense workout begins with circuit 21-15-9.

- Then he performs 21 repetitions of the 2nd ring hold with leg straight.

- Followed by walk plank hold of 21 seconds and inchworms of 21 seconds.

- Next, he performs reverse Superman hold for 21 seconds and 21 planks to push-ups.

- Then he performs 21 lunges. And then in the second round, he performs above exercises for 15 repetitions or seconds and then in the 3rd round he performs above exercises for 9 repetitions or seconds each.

The second day he performs MMA boxing and cardio.

- His cardiovascular training includes long-distance running rowing and cycling.

On the third day, he performs gymnastics and core.

- He starts with warming up by stretching pull-ups, air squats push-ups and jogging for 800m.

- Then he starts circuit training and repeats all the exercises for 5 times.

- He begins with 400m of the run and then follows it by 15 pull-ups and then 25 push-ups.

- Next, he performs 10 handstand push-ups and 5 burpees. (A burpee is done by: Beginning in a standing position; Moving into a squat position with your hands on the ground. (count 1) Kicking your feet back into a plank position, while keeping your arms extended. (count 2) Immediately returning your feet into squat position. (count 3) Standing up from the squat position (count 4).

His fourth and fifth day is an extended part of the above routine.

His Physical Statics.

- He is 6 feet tall and his weight is 177 pounds.

- Chadwick's body type is the mesomorph.(Bodies come in different shapes and sizes. If you have a higher percentage of muscle than body fat, you may have what is known as a mesomorph body type. People with mesomorphic bodies may not have much trouble gaining or losing weight. They may bulk up and maintain muscle mass easily).

- His chest is 42 inches waist is 32 inches and biceps are 16 inches.

- His shoe size is 8.5.

- He has dark brown eyes and black hair.

CHAPTER 7

LET'S GET PERSONAL

Before taking his seat on the Jimmy Kimmel Live! stage, Chadwick Boseman, 40, flashed the Wakanda Forever salute from **Black Panther** to the audience. He had been publicly doing the sign since the immensely popular film released in February 2018. He explained to host Jimmy Kimmel that doing the salute isn't really an option anymore.

'You know what, the funny thing is, if I don't want to do it, I have to not leave the house. I've been chased in cars, I've actually done the scene in Coming to America when he goes to the bathroom and people are bowing to him,' he said.

Chadwick recently wound up the subject of a meme for doing the *Wakanda Forever* salute with less than his usual enthusiasm. Fans online joked that it had transformed from Wakanda Forever to 'Wakanda whatever'.

While his enthusiasm for the salute may or may not be waning, he's surely not tired of those Black Panther checks. The film itself broke box office records, raking in record amounts.

Chadwick Boseman's Net worth and Salary:

Born in 1977, Chadwick Boseman will be 43 years of age in 2020. The South Carolina brought-up Boseman graduated with a directing degree from Howard University in DC. He also attended the British American Drama Academy in London.

Chadwick Boseman has enjoyed success as an actor, playwright, screenwriter and director who has become one of hottest names in Hollywood, after starring in the hit movie 'Black Panther.' The movie, which has broken a number of box office records over the course of its first two months, is Boseman's most successful role to date. Boseman reportedly has a net worth of $8 million dollars. This figure comes from the actor's previous roles, both on TV and on the big screen. Chadwick's estimated net worth figure will certainly increase following the huge success of Black Panther. He reportedly made $700,000 for his first Black

Panther appearance in *Captain America: Civil War*; add that to what he made from movies like *42* and *Gods of Egypt*.

Black Panther surprised Marvel Studios and everyone around the world when it became an international phenomenon. Just hours after the hotly anticipated premiere of "Black Panther," Vanity Fair reported that critics were unified in praise for what's being called Marvel's "first black superhero film." According to Forbes, producers spent $200 million to make the movie and another $150 million to publicize it. Their gamble paid off. "Black Panther" lived up to the hype and then some by grossing $400 million domestically in the first 10 days – the second-fastest behind only "Jurassic World." By the end of February 2018 "Black Panther" had blown past $700 million worldwide to become history's highest-grossing film with a black cast and continued on to make $700,059,566 (domestic) and $646,853,595 (international), TOTALING $1,346,913,161 (worldwide).

Reportedly, Chadwick Boseman made $3 million and Michael B Jordan made $1 million with the first ***Black Panther***. Marvel gets a pass with the first movie. But when ***Black Panther 2*** comes around, they better be ready to cut the checks! It should also be noted that Chadwick signed a 5-movie deal with Marvel, so undoubtedly there will be room or stipulations, negotiations for much better royalties after its release.

Chadwick Boseman is represented by Greene & Associates, Management 360, Viewpoint and Ziffren Brittenham.

Greene & Associates Talent Agency
1901 Avenue of the Stars
Los Angeles, CA 90067
Phone: 310-550-9333

Management 360
9111 Wilshire Blvd
Beverly Hills, CA 90210
310-272-7000

Ziffren Brittenham, LLP
Attorneys at Law
1801 Century Park W
Los Angeles, CA 90067
310- 552-3388

Viewpoint Public Relations
8820 Wilshire Blvd., Ste. 220
Beverly Hills, CA 90211
310-388-3333

Are Wedding Bells in the Works?

Chadwick Boseman has been a movie and TV star for years. But with the release of *Black Panther* — and the film's critical and box office success — he's in the public eye more than ever. This basically means a lot of people talking about whether or not Boseman has a girlfriend, alongside his magnificent acting talent. While the actor is fairly private on social media, there were clues that suggested the *Black Panther* star might be in a relationship.

For quite a while It had been unclear if Chadwick Boseman was married or not. He has, in the past, been spotted wearing a wedding ring, which went missing from his finger. There are clues that suggest that the Black Panther star might be in a relationship, but they were not confirmed. He has not been linked to any possible controversy; and has managed to keep his personal life, personal, away from the bright and somewhat harmful lights of Hollywood.

Boseman was photographed with singer Taylor Simone Ledward at the 2018 NBA All-Star Game in Los Angeles. Of course, the fact that they were seen together didn't prove that they were dating, but a number of tabloids were nevertheless convinced that Boseman and Ledward were an item. One site suggested that the pair might have been dating for as long as a year, though the two of them hadn't confirmed whether or not they were in a relationship and thus could have simply been friends.

The actor was also seen holding hands with a mystery woman in L.A. The woman in the photos was wearing big sunglasses, but, based on the images, it looked like it *could* also be Ledward. Whoever the woman actually was, the pair definitely looked close, while walking down the L.A. streets. Some sites had even reported that Boseman and Ledward were seen together in 2015, though, again, that didn't necessarily mean they had been dating since then.

Chadwick Boseman and 27-year-old singer Taylor Simone Ledward made a rare awards show appearance together at the 2019 SAG Awards, so it was likely that they would walk the carpet together again at the Oscars.

Taylor Simone Ledward is a professional vocalist. She graduated from California State Polytechnic University (Cal Poly), Pomona, in 2014 with a bachelor's degree in music industry studies. Details about Ledward are scarce, but it looks like she has been a member of the music industry for several years, as one fan site noted; she also has an incredible singing voice.

Chadwick & Taylor at the 2019 Oscars

Unfortunately, we probably won't get any details about Boseman's personal life from his Instagram account. He posts on Instagram and Twitter fairly often, but he doesn't share much about his relationships. However, the couple's relationship was made somewhat official by Ledward's *grandmother* in April 2018, when she confirmed the relationship rumors to *In Touch*. Ledward's grandmother told *In Touch*, "She's very happy, and he is, too." But besides being spotted together at a few basketball games, the SAGs and the Oscars, Boseman and Ledward had otherwise kept their relationship pretty private.

Ledward's family seems much more willing to publicly comment on the relationship than the couple themselves. A month before Ledward's grandmother commented on the couple's status, Ledward's sister reportedly clapped back to a fan who posted on social media about shipping Boseman with his *Black Panther* costar, Lupita Nyong'o. BET reported that an account they determined belonged to Ledward's sister commented on an Instagram, "His real life queen is gorgeous, and together they embody true love." She also added, "Not to mention they would make some beautiful babies!"

While BET and *In Touch* had reported that Boseman is happily dating Ledward, the star of *Black Panther* still hadn't actually responded to the family's comments or any other speculation. Not much about Ledward herself is publicly known, either, but multiple sites including *Oprah Magazine* report that she's a singer. Hopefully Boseman's fans will get a chance to get to know his leading lady sometime soon but sharing the specifics of his personal life doesn't exactly seem to be the actor's M.O. ....until a recent headline.... Check this out!

He Put A (Big) Ring on It:
Chadwick Boseman and
Girlfriend Taylor Simone Ledward Are Engaged!.
Chadwick Boseman is Off the Market.

According to a report from "MediaTakeOut", the *Black Panther* actor proposed to longtime love Taylor Simone Ledward during the weekend of October 19, 2019 and she said yes. A source close to her told the site that he popped the question when the couple were on a date in Malibu and they were giddy about the two taking things to the next level in their relationship.

"Chadwick and Simone got engaged," the friend shared. "It was a long time coming and everyone is really happy." Per the source, Taylor and Chadwick are hoping to officially tie the knot in early 2020. And while a rep for the actor had "no comment" for recent engagement rumors, MTO was able to get their hands on photos of Chadwick and Taylor moving about at Tuesday night's Lakers and Clippers game at the Staples Center, and a huge ring can be seen on her finger.

We don't know the official beginning of their relationship, though there is talk that they started dating in either 2015 or 2017. But back in 2018, Taylor's grandmother was actually the one who revealed that the two were an item.

"They respect each other," she told *In Touch Weekly*. "She's very happy and he is, too."

And while Chadwick has been seen out with Taylor for years, he has chosen to remain pretty private about what they have going on. Well, that is until early in 2019 at the NAACP Image Awards, when he publicly shouted her out for the first time.

After winning Outstanding Actor in a Motion Picture, he shared a kiss with Taylor and then got on stage and thanked her for her support.

"Simone, you're with me every day," he said. "I have to acknowledge you right now. Love you."

When cameras panned to her, Taylor sent him a kiss and mouthed, "I love you."

It sounds like they're about to make that love official.

IN CONCLUSION

The Marvel blockbuster *Black Panther* was up for several Academy Awards, including Best Picture, which makes it the first superhero movie to achieve that feat. So, it was pretty much a guarantee that you got to see the whole cast of *Black Panther* don their red-carpet best at the awards show on February 24, 2019...and of course they did...in all their splendor!

The movie scored seven total nominations for the 91st Academy Awards. In addition to its milestone Best Picture nod, *Black Panther* was nominated for Original Score, Original Song ("All the Stars"), Costume Design, Production Design, Sound Editing, and Sound Mixing. *Black Panther* became the first Oscar-winning film from Marvel Studios, taking home three awards - for Costume Design, Production Design, and Original Score, which he had also won a Grammy for earlier.

Costume designer Ruth Carter won her first Oscar, cementing her place in Oscar history, as the first African American woman to win in the category. Bringing home the Oscar for Production Design were the duo of Jay Hart and Hannah Beachler, who became the first African-American to be nominated for - and win - in this category. And Ludwig Goransson won his first Oscar for BLACK PANTHER's original score (which he also won a Grammy for mere days ago!) In his speech, Goransson thanked the film's director Ryan Coogler, with whom he was a student at USC.

Chadwick Boseman already has ideas for what to do after *Black Panther*. Originally a screenwriter, Boseman told *Rolling Stone* that he and his writing partner Logan Coles are working on the script for a new movie that *Moonlight*'s Barry Jenkins will direct. "There's a plethora of stories in our culture that haven't been told, because Hollywood didn't believe they were viable," the actor told *Rolling Stone*. If *Black Panther* is any indication, though, there's definitely a cultural appetite for more stories about African Americans.

ABOUT THE AUTHOR

Tony Rose is an NAACP Image Award Winner for Outstanding Literature. He is also the publisher of Amber and Colossus Books. He has published numerous biographies, including: **Nikki Minaj; Jay-Z; Beyonce; Tupac** and **Suge Knight;** as well as historical books *Obama Talks Back – Global Lessons, A Dialogue with Today's Young Leaders* and *Tracing Our Roots*; He has also written numerous books, including:

African American History in the United States of America; An Autobiography of an American Ghetto Boy; America - The Black Point of View and *How to Be in the Entertainment Business.* (www.amberbookspublishing.com)